FICTION

by

Steven Dietz

SAMUEL FRENCH, INC.

45 West 25th Street   7623 Sunset Boulevard
NEW YORK 10010   HOLLYWOOD 90046
LONDON   *TORONTO*

IMPORTANT BILLING AND CREDIT REQUIREMENTS

FICTION was originally produced in New York City by
Roundabout Theatre Company
Todd Haimes, Artistic Director

FICTION was orginally produced by
McCarter Theatre, Princeton, NJ
Emily Mann, Artistic Director/Jeffery Woodward, Managing Director

FICTION was orginally commissioned and produced
in a workshop setting by ACT Theatre, Seattle, WA

This production was originally produced with the assistance of
The Kennedy Center Fund for New American Plays

ROUNDABOUT THEATRE COMPANY

TODD HAIMES, Artistic Director
ELLEN RICHARD, Managing Director
JULIA C. LEVY, Executive Director, External Affairs

Presents

Tom Irwin   Julie White

in

fiction

by

Steven Dietz

with

Emily Bergl

Set Design	*Costume Design*	*Lighting Design*	*Original Music & Sound*
James Youmans	David C. Woolard	Jeff Croiter	John Gromada

Production Stage Manager	*Production Managers*	*Casting by*
Jay Adler	Kai Brothers	Mele Nagler
	Bridget Markov	

General Manager	*Founding Director*	*Associate Artistic Director*
Don-Scott Cooper	Gene Feist	Scott Ellis

Press Representative	*Director of Marketing*
Boneau/Bryan-Brown	David B. Steffen

Directed by

David Warren

Fiction was originally commissioned and produced in a workshop setting by ACT Theatre, Seattle, WA
Fiction was originally produced by McCarter Theatre, Princeton, N.J.
Emily Mann, Artistic Director/Jeffrey Woodward, Managing Director
Roundabout Theatre Company is a member of the League of Resident Theatres. www.roundabouttheatre.org

Fiction was commissioned and first presented in a worshop setting by ACT Theatre, Seattle, Washington, in March, 2002. The stage manager was Michael Chemers. It was directed by the author. The cast was as follows:

LINDA WATERMAN   Barbara Dirickson
MICHAEL WATERMAN   Stephen Godwin
ABBY DRAKE   Suzanne Bouchard

Fiction received its world premiere at the McCarter Theatre Center (Emily Mann, Artistic Director; Jeffrey Woodward, Managing Director), Princeton, New Jersey, in April, 2003. It was directed by David Warren. The set design was by James M. Youmans, the costume design by David Woolard, the lighting design by Donald Holder, the sound design and original music was by John Gromada. The dramaturg was Liz Engelman. The producing director was Mara Isaacs. The stage manager was Alison Cote. The cast was as follows:

LINDA WATERMAN   Laila Robins
MICHAEL WATERMAN   Robert Cuccioli
ABBY DRAKE   Marianne Hagan

CAST

LINDA WATERMAN... a woman in her mid-forties.
MICHAEL WATERMAN... her husband, same age.
ABBY DRAKE... a woman in her mid-thirties.

*Note: Though all the characters will also play
themselves as much as twenty years younger, a
change in physcial appearance is neither called for
nor encouraged.*

TIME AND PLACE

The present and before. Various American cities.
And Paris.

SETTING

A table, a desk, and a few chairs. Nothing more.

"The power to change one's life comes from a
paragraph, a lone remark."
-- James Salter, *Light Years*

ACKNOWLEDGEMENTS

The author wishes to also thank the following individuals and organizations who contributed to the creation and development of *Fiction:*

Andie Miller
Dr. Katie O'Farrell
Jim Leonard, Jr.
The John F. Kennedy Center Fund for New American Plays
Patricia Clarkson
John Slattery
Gretchen Egolf
Suzanne Bouchard
John Procaccino
Emily Cedergreen
Scott Weldin
Rick Paulsen
Carolyn Keim
Eric Chappelle
Jeffrey K. Hanson
Kurt Beattie
ACT Theatre, Seattle
Rick Seer
Old Globe Theatre, San Diego
Tracy Brigden
City Theatre Company, Pittsburgh

Allison Gregory - my wife, best critic, and greatest collaborator.

for Liz Engelman

ACT ONE

*(A **Cafe Table.** MICHAEL and LINDA sit across from each other. They are well into a heated discussion. And they are having a wonderful time.)*

LINDA. No, that is not the point, that is not the point at all —
MICHAEL. The point? Why does there need to be a point?
LINDA. Michael —
MICHAEL. Welcome to the land of the Great Reductivity —
LINDA. That's not a word.
MICHAEL. The Great Reductiveness —
LINDA. *Reductivism.*
MICHAEL — in which everything we say must be shrunk down to You Make A Point and I Refute It; I Make A Statement and You Rebut It. Is this really the best we can do?
LINDA. Do you ever hear yourself —
MICHAEL. God help us.
LINDA. — No, really, do you ever just step outside your body and *let your mouth talk?* Because it would, you know. I assure you, your mouth would keep talking even if you were away in another room, another state —

(He is laughing now.)

9

LINDA. *(Cont'd.)* It is clearly, as they say, a machine that will "go of itself" —

MICHAEL. I'm not laughing with you, I'm laughing at you.

LINDA. Because if you did that, even once, if you heard the actual words that come out of your mouth — I'm convinced that you would stop and weep —

MICHAEL. Weep, Linda? I would weep?

LINDA. *(Overlapping.)* — You would cry the tears of a man who has made his way through the world on nothing but bluster and hyperbole —

MICHAEL. Oh, that's good, that's very good —

LINDA. And having done so, and having realized the extent to which his life is so clearly an empty shell, a barren wasteland —

MICHAEL. Loving the metaphors —

LINDA. A frozen tundra —

MICHAEL. Mix me up another one —

LINDA. An endless desert of aching regret —

MICHAEL. *(Applauding.)* Ah, bravo!

LINDA. *(Overlapping.)* At that moment. You. Yes, you, Michael. You would weep.

(He stares at her, transfixed.)

LINDA. *(Cont'd.)* And it just might look damn good on you.

(She stares at him. They sip their coffees.)

MICHAEL. I forget what started that.
LINDA. Me, too.
MICHAEL. Oh, well.

(They sip their coffees.)

FICTION

LINDA. "Piece of My Heart."

MICHAEL. You're still wrong.

LINDA. I will grant you that "Twist and Shout" was Lennon's best vocal work —

MICHAEL. Oh, John and I thank you for that.

LINDA. And, hey, just parenthetically —

MICHAEL. Oh, good, for a moment I thought you might finish one of your sentences.

LINDA. Why is it that you can't just sit at a cafe and chat? I mean, god forbid, we talk about the weather, the food, the museums and cathedrals.

MICHAEL. And say what? "Europe, man — it's really old."

LINDA. There always has to be a game — why is that? Do you know what that says about you?

MICHAEL. I feel certain you'll tell me.

LINDA. And, do you know how instantly unattractive that makes you? I mean, most men have to grow a mustache to ruin their appeal, but not you.

MICHAEL. Are we closing in on our point here?

LINDA. On our *point?*

MICHAEL. Yeah, can we smell the barn, yet?

LINDA. The point here is your supreme reliance upon the most shallow of things —

MICHAEL. Oh, right.

LINDA. This covetous grip you have upon the facile and mundane.

MICHAEL. Touch?

LINDA. I mean, really, Michael: what are you so afraid of?!

MICHAEL. I'm AFRAID that you'll never answer my QUESTION!

LINDA. The Greatest Rock and Roll Performance —

MICHAEL. Vocal —

LINDA. Vocal Performance —

MICHAEL. Ever.

LINDA. The key word being EVER.

MICHAEL. John Lennon. "Twist and Shout." Case closed.

LINDA. *(To no one in particular.)* Check, please!

MICHAEL. I mean, sure, right, there are runners-up galore: Mick Jagger, "Honky Tonk Woman" —

MICHAEL.
(Cont'd.) Roger Daltry, "Won't Get Fooled Again" — Rod Stewart, "Maggie Mae" — Joe Cocker, "Feelin' Alright" —

LINDA.
What is this thing you have for British rock stars? You're — what? — the world's foremost Anglophile Groupie?!

MICHAEL. *(Cont'd.)* — but when push comes to shove and you're well into your cups at your fifth bar of the night and bumming a smoke from a man who just blew his nose on the window — at that moment, when your head is nothing but smoke and lies and noise — at that moment you want ONE SONG to come on — and when it does, and when you yell at the bartender to *crank that fucker up so the angels can hear* it — that song — the way that man sings that song — will yank your heels up through the top of your head and make your guts dance on the ceiling.

LINDA. *(Ala Janis.)* Come on ...

MICHAEL. That song is "Twist and Shout."

LINDA. Come on ...

MICHAEL. That man is John Lennon.

LINDA. Come on ...

MICHAEL. And this case is closed.

LINDA. *(Standing.)* ... and TAKE IT. TAKE ANOTHER LITTLE PIECE OF MY HEART NOW BABY ...

(She hums/riffs on the song, as —)

MICHAEL. Linda — please sit down —

LINDA. Oh, let 'em stare. The French love to stare. Ask anyone.

MICHAEL. Really, Linda, I mean it —

FICTION

LINDA. Ca vous amuse, no? Je suis L'Americaine lunatique!

MICHAEL. Would you please —

LINDA. *(Instantly back in her chair, right in his face.)* Have you HEARD "Piece of My Heart"? Do you live in the *known world?* Are you really so gapingly out of touch, so fundamentally unaware that Janis Joplin could — with one burst of music out of that throat of hers — actually *set your house on fire?!*

MICHAEL. It's an impressive performance. I grant you that.

LINDA. A good créme brulée is impressive. This, Michael, is EARTH-SHATTERING.

MICHAEL. *(Holding out his palm.)* Seems to be raining hyperbole.

LINDA. And I don't even LIKE Janis Joplin. If I never see another clip of her shoving a bottle of Southern Comfort into those pouty blue lips it will be too soon. But, here's the thing:

MICHAEL. *(Looking away, for the waiter.)* Oh, good. The thing.

LINDA. I for one am able to set aside my own personal tastes — this would be a good place for you to start listening, it may have special resonance for you — I am able to look beyond my own whims and wishes and see the TRUTH.

MICHAEL. The Truth — I am healed!

LINDA. *(Overlapping.)* I am able to recognize that that woman, in that song, took something from the air and made it flesh and blood and bone. She sang that song and — fuck it all — that song *stayed sung.*

MICHAEL. Nicely put.

LINDA. Thank you.

MICHAEL. And you're still wrong.

LINDA. I GIVE UP.

MICHAEL. But, you're wrong in all the right ways.

LINDA. See there! That's your trick, over and over —

MICHAEL. Another coffee?

LINDA. You're the master of the coda, you know that? The tidy, definitive conceit.

MICHAEL. I take that as —

FICTION

LINDA. It's not a compliment.
MICHAEL. Okay. I don't —
LINDA. It's an observation.
MICHAEL. Got it.
LINDA. What time is it?
MICHAEL. Nearly five.
LINDA. You're kidding.

(He shakes his head "no." She looks at him. Takes a deep breath.)

LINDA. *(Cont'd.)* Well. Where did the afternoon go?
MICHAEL. Nowhere.

(Beat. He smiles.)

LINDA. Yes.

(Beat. She smiles.)

MICHAEL. Nowhere at all.
LINDA. Well. *(Simply.)* Nice to meet you.
MICHAEL. Nice to meet you, too.

(They shake hands, quick and friendly. And she goes. MICHAEL turns and speaks to the audience.)

MICHAEL. *(Cont'd.)* And she was gone. I went back to my room, just off the Boulevard Saint Germain, and I wrote these words in my journal: "achingly vibrant." "I met a woman today at a cafe on the Rue Cler. This woman ... she was achingly vibrant. And I fear I will never see her again." Or so I thought. I'd always thought that's what I'd written. Recently, however — for reasons that will become clear — I went back and read the actual words I scribbled on that fateful day: "Late lunch.

FICTION

Too cold for a walk. Tomorrow, the Louvre." We remember our diaries as works of art. And that they remain, cloistered in the museum of our own nostalgia, until we make that great grand mistake: until we read them. Of a man and his memory — memory is the better writer.

*(A **Classroom.** LINDA addresses the audience as her students.)*

LINDA. Welcome, suckers, to a class in creative writing. My name is Linda Waterman.

MICHAEL. Her given name is Belinda. It's a name I like much more than she does. I like that initial plosive consonant — the delicious bravado of the letter "b" — introducing, like a good ringmaster or maitre d' — the alluring "l" which waits just around the corner. "Belinda." Fanciful and purposeful. Like drinks before dinner.

LINDA. This class is called the Advanced Fiction Workshop. That name is a lie. I cannot teach you to write. Or, more to the point, I can only teach you to write *like me*. And, believe me, you don't want to do that. Oh, sure, you might get one good book out — but that one book will expose all your tricks and writerly shenanigans, and when your daring and important and inevitably flawed sophomore effort hits the shelves you will be caught out as the "one-trick pony" you most feared you'd become. Your stock will fall. Your reputation will be remaindered. And you will stand here, like me, right now — trying very hard not to punish your students for the inequities of art.

(Calls on an unseen student.)

LINDA. *(Cont'd.)* Yes? Question? *(Beat.)* The earnest young man with aspirations to facial hair has asked if my husband, Michael Waterman — the noted and successful author — will be coming in to speak to this class. *(Smiles.)* I certainly hope not.

MICHAEL. To all who know her — including her students — she is "Linda." When I dare to ask why she loathes her given name, she throws me a look — there are, you know, entire *novels* in women's looks — and this look says: "Do you really want to wade into the maelstrom here, honey?" And that's all I need to hear. A marriage, however good, is not a "tell-all" enterprise. It is a pact between necessary strangers. So, I change the subject, fix her some tea, and we skip over it like a stone.

LINDA. *(To her class.)* I've been asked to use my own first novel — "At The Cape" — as a text for this class. I presume you've all read it and that you are in my debt for its relative brevity. "At The Cape" is based on a trip I made to South Africa in my early twenties. A vacation that turned dangerous; that led to the arrest of an innocent young man. A trip that changed my life forever.

MICHAEL. She has been my wife now for twenty years. We have written, eaten, fought, loved, laughed, bickered, mourned, traveled, celebrated and wept together — side by side — for most of our adult lives. She is everything to me. And, if the doctors are to be believed, in three weeks she will be dead.

*(**Home**. LINDA turns to MICHAEL.)*

LINDA. Why must they do it in weeks? I mean: do people really want that? Three weeks, three years — what is the appeal here? I'd like them to do it in, say, meals: "You have at least twenty really good dinners left." Or: "You have endured your last public radio pledge week. Congratulations."

MICHAEL. *(To audience.)* The medical term is "Sphenoid Wing Meningioma."

LINDA. Like something out of Nabokov —

MICHAEL. For a writer like my wife —

LINDA. Some demented butterfly.

MICHAEL. — A writer who prizes economy of language, it is a dreadfully *floral* affliction.

LINDA. You know, call me old fashioned, but "brain tumor" is just good enough for me.

MICHAEL. That was one week ago —

LINDA. Remember that one doctor I liked?

MICHAEL. — Following a seizure that landed her in the emergency room.

LINDA. You know why I liked him? Because while everyone else was talking about "an enhancing lesion, corrupting the anterior right temporal fossa in a pear tree —"

MICHAEL. She was admitted —

LINDA. This guy —

MICHAEL. Prepped —

LINDA. My straight shooter —

MICHAEL. And wheeled away.

LINDA. He just looked me in the eyes and said: "Size of a plum, dear. Stuck there in your head."

MICHAEL. A "pterional craniotomy" was performed.

LINDA. I love that: "performed." Like maybe people will *applaud.*

MICHAEL. This procedure removed as much of the tumor as was deemed safe. And the rest —

LINDA. They just leave it in there!

MICHAEL. *(Turns to her, calmly.)* They don't just "leave it in there."

LINDA. Well, they don't take it out!

MICHAEL. *(To audience.)* It's called Stereotactic Radiation Therapy

LINDA. And that Brocky — that Blocky or Brocky thing —

MICHAEL. "Brachytherapy" —

LINDA. What a weird-ass thing THAT is. Sending in these tiny radiated paratroopers —

MICHAEL. "Seeds", honey. They call them seeds.

LINDA. This little *cranial jihad* whose job is to what, really?!

MICHAEL. *(To audience.)* "Interstitial radiation."

LINDA. It's like your head is being colonized. That one intern actually used "Pac Man" as an example. *(Illustrates with her hand.)* Chomp-chomp-chomp! Tumor gone — you win!

FICTION

(Silence.)

MICHAEL. The first thing her surgeon told us was that ninety-five percent of these kinds of tumors are benign. Still dangerous, of course, but benign. The pathology report came back today.

LINDA. *(Quietly.)* "Remarkable." He actually said that word.

MICHAEL. Not hers.

LINDA. "Ms. Waterman, I must tell you —"

MICHAEL. Hers is malignant.

LINDA. "This is remarkable."

(Silence. They look at one another.)

MICHAEL. The way he told you. It was awful.

LINDA. Very studied, didn't you think? The clenched brow, the eager posture. Something straight out of a medical school primer: "Dropping the Bomb on Your Patient" — but all I could really focus on was his lips. And from those lips... that wonderfully sibilant "s." The word "sorry" — as sibilant as I've ever heard it — a low breeze off the ocean — beautiful, really. *(Beat.)* "Sorry." "Serious." "Seldom seen someone survive."

(Silence.)

LINDA. *(Cont'd. Quietly, edge of tears.)* Michael ...

(He goes to her.)

LINDA. *(Cont'd.)* I need some lies.

MICHAEL. Honey, I don't —

LINDA. I need some big fat whopping lies about the fallibility of Western medicine — anything you've got along those lines would be

FICTION

great — and I also need ridiculous stories about miracle cures — like that friend of your agent who had a tumor the size of "a Roma tomato" — not just any tomato, mind you, *a Roma* — and she packed up her little internal vegetable and she took it to that place in Finland where they treated it with mistletoe — with fucking MISTLETOE — and what happened, Michael? Do you remember what happened?!

MICHAEL. It worked.

LINDA. IT WORKED. Deck the halls. Hallelujah.

(Silence.)

LINDA. *(Cont'd. Simply.)* I'm leaving you my diaries. A huge box of them. Sorry. Not organized in the least. Sorry. You've never read a word of them — *(A gentle accusation.)* — as far as I know.

MICHAEL. Never once.

LINDA. But all these years — they've been right here. You know where I keep them, I'm sure. Behind the —

MICHAEL. Next to the —

LINDA. Right. In that old apple box. When I'm gone, I want you to read them. Will you do that?

MICHAEL. *(Pause.)* Linda, we're going to be okay —

LINDA. *(Overlapping.)* It's ludicrous — it really is, Michael — not to mention vain — I mean vain in a truly Tom Wolfe-ian sort of way — to think that they are not *real*, that *I* am not *real* unless someone reads them. *(Beat.)* And they're boring. Sorry. Really boring. Boring in the "Today I saw a robin on the lawn" manner. If you wanted excitement, you should have married Plath or Nin or Stendahl — because mine are boring.

MICHAEL. Listen to me —

LINDA. And this is so gutless, I know — completely without honor — to make sure I'm safely the hell out of this world before I let you open those pages. Sorry. *(Pause.)* God, I'm hungry. Let's eat one of those twenty meals.

(She moves away.)

MICHAEL. *(Gently.)* I would have, anyway, you know. *(Beat.)* Read them.
LINDA. Still. I had to ask.
MICHAEL. I understand.
LINDA. And one thing more.
MICHAEL. Anything.
LINDA. I want to read yours.

(He looks at her.)

LINDA. *(Cont'd.)* Before I go. I want to read your journals. *(Pause.)* You're not saying anything.
MICHAEL. It just, you know, just —
LINDA. Surprised you?
MICHAEL. Well —
LINDA. Sure.
MICHAEL. I mean —
LINDA. But, it's only fair, right? *(Pause.)* Mr. Waterman — are you there?
MICHAEL. Sure. I mean, of course. Of course you can. Now? You want them now? They're under my —
LINDA. Inside that old —
MICHAEL. Right.
LINDA. No —
MICHAEL. Hmm?
LINDA. Not tonight.
MICHAEL. Okay.
LINDA. You hate this.
MICHAEL. No, I just —
LINDA. We don't have to do it.

FICTION

MICHAEL. Linda —

LINDA. I mean, do we? Should they — what? — should these words just *vanish?* And, if they're that disposable — *who on earth were they ever for?* For my family? — to confirm things about me they already know they can't stand? For some earnest young grad student looking for the "missing pieces", the "lingering mysteries" of my flash-in-the-pan, dead-before-her-time career as a writer of fiction? For the child we never had?

(This lands.)

MICHAEL. *(Simply.)* They're for us.
LINDA. Do you ever read yours?
MICHAEL. No.
LINDA. Nor do I. So who are they for?
MICHAEL. They are ...
LINDA. Yes?
MICHAEL. They just *are.*

(Silence.)

LINDA. Sorry.
MICHAEL. What?
LINDA. Forget it. Bad idea.
MICHAEL. Linda —

LINDA. Stupid of me — really — what a thing to be doing, when I could be gorging myself on créme brulée with impunity.

MICHAEL. I warn you.

LINDA. Yes?

MICHAEL. You think yours are boring... *(Points to himself.)* Worse. Much worse. And hard to read. Too many dark rooms, crappy pens, excellent whiskey.

LINDA. So ... this is okay?

FICTION

MICHAEL. Not at all —

LINDA. Then —

MICHAEL. — but it's what you want. I assumed you'd read them. Some day when I was long gone. I always thought I'd knock off in my fifties and you'd take up with some kid in khakis half my age. "Brent" or "Trevor" or "Josh." And on some rainy night — when Young Mr. Khaki was off doing volunteer work — you'd light a fire, pour yourself a good cabernet and hunker down with my past. I hoped if I was dead and gone, you might find a way to forgive me.

LINDA. For what?

MICHAEL. None of us — given a good hard look — can fail to disappoint.

(MICHAEL goes. LINDA speaks to the audience.)

LINDA. When I came down for breakfast the next morning, there was the box — a wooden ship's box, circa 1905 — sitting in the room. Waiting for me.

(MICHAEL appears, putting on a coat.)

MICHAEL. I'm going out.

LINDA. Okay.

MICHAEL. Just, you know —

LINDA. Good morning.

MICHAEL. — out.

LINDA. How'd you sleep?

MICHAEL. I made one more entry, last night, after you went to bed. They're all there. Arranged chronologically and numbered accordingly. There's an index — laminated and affixed to the lid on the inside. (Beat.) It's pretty self-explanatory.

LINDA. I see.

MICHAEL. But I can't be here. Is that —

FICTION

LINDA. Right.

MICHAEL.
I mean, you know what it's like when I read your stories — you can't bear to watch me doing it — it's agonizing — that's your word — sitting there trying not to read my face for evidence of what I'm thinking —

LINDA.
I completely — *(Beat.)* Michael — right, you're right — *(Beat.)* It's fine — really — *(Beat.)* You don't have to explain —

(Silence.)

MICHAEL. So ... I'm gonna go. You need anything?
LINDA. No.
MICHAEL. You took your pills?
LINDA. Yes.
MICHAEL. Even the —
LINDA. Yes, even the one I hate.
MICHAEL. Good — okay —
LINDA. Michael —
MICHAEL. I made your tea. It's in there.
LINDA. Thank you.
MICHAEL. And I'll have my cell, if you need to —
LINDA. *Michael?*
MICHAEL. What?
LINDA. Good morning.
MICHAEL. *(Pause.)* Morning.

(He goes. She stares at the box. Does not open it. Turns, instead, to the audience.)

LINDA. I took one writing class in college. My professor was an angry, but evolving ex-radical. A goddess-worshipping feminist with hairy pits and two hundred dollar shoes. A fish adamantly without a bicycle. I remember the African totems she wore on a chain around her neck — dangling there like errant climbers over the ample ledge of her breasts. She had us write our names on tiny pieces of paper — then she burned them and gave us each new names. Mine was "Oraluna." She took away our pencils and paper and made us walk around the campus feeling the trees. We chanted and drummed and took deep breaths that would "unshackle the cowering angels within us." And, to her credit, a lot of us had *really good sex* — but nobody wrote a damn thing. *(Pause.)* Years later I saw her in a bathroom at a local bar. Piss-drunk on gin. She'd published a memoir to good notices — about her daring travels in Africa, India, Southeast Asia. I hadn't read it, but said congrats and helped her wipe the lipstick off her teeth. I told her I hoped to have some adventures of my own, now that I was out of school. She leaned forward. Put her mouth to my ear: "Remember baby: the lies begin when we lift the pen." *(Pause.)* She was dead within the year. A warm bath; a slit in each wrist. And her diaries confirmed what many had suspected: She'd invented it all. Cobbled it together from other people's books. She'd never traveled, had no adventures to speak of. She'd sat in her sweat pants at her ex-husband's guest house — typing away, as the live-in cook brought her figs and bruschetta. *(Pause.)* Upon her death, of course, sales of her book tripled.

(LINDA stares, once again, at the box.)

MICHAEL. I killed a couple hours — then I had to call. There was no answer. Do I rush home? Do I leave her be? I had no idea. I hadn't left her alone since she was diagnosed. I called again. No answer. The panic descended.

LINDA. The third time the phone rang I answered. It was my doctor. He had sent the pathology report to another lab — and, again, the malignancy was confirmed. What's more: the lab said my results presented "variables" they had never seen. Could they use my case in their oncology department? Would I mind — he wondered out loud on the phone — if my death was *taught?*

MICHAEL. Linda's novel, "At the Cape", is the story of a young American girl who spends an amorous night with a young black man from the townships. His name is Simon. He is a drummer. She has gone to a *shabeen* in Soweto to hear his band. Driving home, late at night, middle of nowhere — they are chased by two men — white Afrikaners — who run their car off the road. Simon is beaten and tied to the back of the truck — forced to watch as the young woman is raped and left for dead. Simon is framed for this crime and sent to prison. *(Pause.)* The young woman survives. And she makes her way to the Cape. She stands there, on a cliff, at the tip of Africa. A place called "False Bay." She looks out at the water. To her left, the Indian ocean. To her right, the Atlantic. And in the distance, remarkably, she sees ... a line. A line of white water, trailing off to the horizon. Certain it's a trick of the light, she asks a local what she's seeing: "The meeting of the waves. That place where two worlds collide." As the novel ends, the young woman is leaning over the edge of the cliff — on the verge, it seems, of taking her own life. *(Pause.)* It is a moment my wife wrote not from imagination, but from *memory.* Because she was that woman.

(LINDA now lifts the lid, opens the box. It is filled with an orderly array of identical, black journals. She reaches inside. Removes a journal. Speaks to the audience.)

LINDA. Where to begin? I needed something simple. Just to ease me in. So, I reached back over what I thought would be a vague but appropriate number of years — toward quote, unquote: "simpler times."

(LINDA opens the journal and reads.)

LINDA. *(Cont'd.)* "Twenty-six June. The Drake Colony."

FICTION

*(A **Cottage.** MICHAEL appears, a book bag over his shoulder. He sets it down on a desk, and unpacks it, during the following. LINDA reads/looks on throughout.)*

MICHAEL. Well, they've called my bluff. One applies to these writer's colonies claiming a desperate need for time to write, time to be alone and create in seclusion, untethered from the world's random, rampant noise. And, god, the thought of that — how delicious. And the letter of acceptance — how gratifying. And the packing of bags, the selecting of the proper pens and note pads and relevant books, a favorite old sweater, a photo or two — how lovely the preparations; how rich the goodbyes. And the flight — the lovely ladies gracing your tray with peanuts — the person next to you falling straightaway into your trap, asking "what brings you out this way?" — and you answer, dropping the name of the Colony like a pearl, and you watch as the romance of your own life flowers there in a stranger's eyes. You arrive into a sea of smiles and chatter; young interns just *aching* to carry your bags. And you are taken to your cottage, made ready and to your liking. And you close the door behind you — the welcoming room encasing you in its thick, resonant, tomb-like silence. *(Pause.)* And now you know. Now, you get it. These fuckers expect you to WRITE SOMETHING. Didn't they know you were kidding?! No matter what they say, writers don't want to write — they just want to "be writers." Throw us a party. Pour us a drink. Surround us with grad students and divorcées and let us talk about how desperately we need our precious solitude — but FOR GOD'S SAKE, DON'T STICK US WITH IT!

(MICHAEL sits at the desk. Stares front.)

LINDA. I had been there two years before. Working on my first novel: "At the Cape." The one that just *sang.* A hard story that came out easy and right and found its public and garnered awards and made me

FICTION

important and desireable and arrogant as hell. The book that just flat-out *worked.* I was asked to recommend other writers to the Colony. And based on nothing more than that — Michael hadn't published a word, yet — they invited my husband.

(ABBY appears. Dressed casually. Carrying a three-ring binder.)

    ABBY. Mr. Waterman?

(MICHAEL turns.)

    ABBY. *(Cont'd.)* Is that right? Cottage Four. Michael Waterman?
    MICHAEL. That's me.
    ABBY. Hi.
    MICHAEL. Hi.
    ABBY. You got here okay?
    MICHAEL. No, I'm still at the airport. Can you call me a cab?

(Silence.)

    ABBY. I'm Abby.
    MICHAEL. You could laugh, you know. At a person's first bad joke. Even a snicker — just to be polite.
    ABBY. *(Beat, brightly.)* Ha.
    MICHAEL. Thank you.
    ABBY. Welcome to the —
    MICHAEL. They don't get better, by the way.
    ABBY. Sorry?
    MICHAEL. My jokes.
    ABBY. Oh, that's okay. I've seen a hundred writers come through here and not one of them could tell a joke to save their life. Now —
    MICHAEL. Oh, but I bet you can. Late at night at the local bar — there is a local bar around here, right?, I mean we're not on some kind of

"Outward Bound" thing, right? — we are still, I trust, in proximate contact with the civilizing influence of distilled beverages?

(ABBY just stares at him.)

    MICHAEL. *(Cont'd.) Is there hootch nearby?*
    ABBY. There's a bar. Two bars, actually.
    MICHAEL. And I bet you just slay 'em there. You just seem ...
    ABBY. Yes?
    MICHAEL. *(Pause, more quietly.)* ... like you could.

(She gives him a long look. Then, once again, she adopts her "welcoming" tone. Hands him the binder.)

    ABBY. Welcome to the Drake Colony. For your information, a brief history of the Colony is printed in this binder, as well as a list of other writers who have occupied this cottage. Breakfast and Dinner are communal — held in the main lodge, called "Poppy's House" around here —
    MICHAEL. Why is it called —
    ABBY. It's all in the binder. Lunch is delivered to your door each day. If there's anything else you need — please don't hesitate to ask. On behalf of everyone here at the Drake, we hope your stay is a good and productive one. Any questions?

(He shakes his head "no.")

    ABBY. *(Cont'd.)* Happy writing.

(And she is gone. MICHAEL stares off after her.)

    MICHAEL. *(A journal entry.)* Her name .. is Abby. And as she walks away, I know that whatever the future may hold, *I will invent her forever.*

FICTION

(Pause.) I see her there ...

LINDA. *(Reading, sharing the overlapped lines.)* "... there, in Venice, holding court amid the canals, tossing back her hair like whiskey."

MICHAEL. I see her there, in Madrid, in the sweet gloom of winter, surrounded by a dozen men destined to stumble away with nothing —

LINDA. "— with nothing but her name on their lips; that lethal combination of beauty, danger, youth and wit."

MICHAEL. I see her there, in Paris, eyes peering from a window. She has been up all night, it seems, commiserating with a friend. But now she throws on a black sweater and steps into the street — all weary and poised and *unforgettable.*

LINDA. "She is all a man will ever know of the life he failed to live." *(Pause.)* And then, under this, he writes:

MICHAEL. *(A sarcastic laugh.)* What a lot of SHIT. All hail the imposter. You big large enormous awful fucking lying FAKE. Do something productive —

LINDA. "Bag groceries."

MICHAEL. Build a chair.

LINDA. *(Smiles.)* "Leave the writing to your wife."

*(**Home.** MICHAEL turns to her. His mood is upbeat.)*

MICHAEL. I brought you some lunch. Should I bring it in?

(She closes the journal in her hand.)

LINDA. You were going to go.
MICHAEL. I did.
LINDA. Out. You were going.
MICHAEL. I went.
LINDA. But —
MICHAEL. And I'm back. I went and I'm back.
LINDA. I was reading.

FICTION

MICHAEL. Yes.

LINDA. I mean, I'm still —

MICHAEL. Right. I know that. But I decided I was being an idiot. Trying to not be here. I'm sure it struck you as a little — I don't know — just a little foolish, a little absurd for me to run away like that.

LINDA. I liked it.

MICHAEL. Okay.

LINDA. Could you go?

MICHAEL. Linda —

LINDA. I liked it. It's better. You should go.

MICHAEL. Well — okay — but I —

LINDA. All these weeks you've been taking care of me — I know you've wanted to be out — go to your bookstores, catch a movie, have a beer — and you couldn't, 'cause you had to be here with me —

MICHAEL. I wanted to be here —

LINDA. Yes, I know, but now you don't have to be — now you can do those things —

MICHAEL. I don't want to do those things —

LINDA. Yes, I know, but *could you?* Could you just *do them* — or something — whatever it is you do when you're not doing everything for me — could you please DO THAT for the rest of the day? Tonight, too. And maybe tomorrow — depending on how long it takes me to plow through these books.

MICHAEL. Okay, already —

LINDA. When you read mine you'll be alone.

(Silence.)

MICHAEL. I'll have my cell.

LINDA. Okay.

MICHAEL. If you need anything —

LINDA. I'll be fine.

MICHAEL. But if you do.

FICTION

LINDA. Right.
MICHAEL. Okay. I'm going. *(Beat.)* Sorry.
LINDA. For?
MICHAEL. I don't know. Just a floating "sorry." Use as needed.
LINDA. Okay.
MICHAEL. Bye.
LINDA. Michael.
MICHAEL. Hmm?
LINDA. It's okay. This is okay. This is not bad. I just —
MICHAEL. Got it.
LINDA. Okay.
MICHAEL. Right.
LINDA. Bye.
MICHAEL. One thing.

(He goes to the wooden box. Looks quickly at the laminated index. Finds the journal he wants. Opens it. Pages through it for a moment. Stops, having found the page he wants. He tears this single page out of the journal. Folds it. Puts it in a pocket. Puts the journal back in its place. He hides none of this from LINDA. He turns back to her. Chipper.)

MICHAEL. *(Cont'd.)* Okay. It's okay.

(He goes. She turns to the audience.)

LINDA. Do I know every word that was spoken? Every glance and gesture; the feel of every room? No. *(Beat.)* But I know *him. (Lifting a journal.)* And because of that, it takes only a sentence to conjure a scene. A single phrase, scribbled in a margin, gives mortar enough to build an entire day.

*(She turns a page and continues reading. **A Bar.** MICHAEL appears,*

holding a beer. Looking around.)

MICHAEL. *(Looking off.)* It's Abby, right? Over here. It's me.

(ABBY approaches. Just to be polite. She, too, has a beer.)

ABBY. Good evening, Mr. Waterman.
MICHAEL. Michael. Mike. Mikey. Mickey. *(Beat.)* Hi.
ABBY. You found your hootch.
MICHAEL. With your help. *(Looking around.)* A cordial, if unpre-possessing, little watering hole.

(As before, ABBY just stares at him.)

MICHAEL. *(Cont'd.)* Nice bar.

(She nods.)

MICHAEL. *(Cont'd.)* A little run-in with the barkeep — nothing serious — I just won't drink a beer that's in a green bottle. Only brown. Brown for beer. Green for wine. Clear for other spirits. Just a little something I believe.
ABBY. *(Nods.)* See you later.

(She starts out.)

MICHAEL. Hey, I read that binder. Just like you told me to. You put a lot of work into that.
ABBY. An intern did it. Years ago. We update it every now and then.
MICHAEL. I see.
ABBY. I'm glad it was helpful.
MICHAEL. Just one problem, though.
ABBY. I don't mean to be rude, but —

FICTION

ABBY
(Cont'd.) I'm with some friends over here — so, if it could wait till morning —

MICHAEL.
Oh, right, you're off the clock — I completely understand —

MICHAEL. You run along and have fun —

ABBY. I'd ask you to join us —

MICHAEL. Oh, I'd just embarrass you. Drink too much, insult your friends — *(Waving, calling off.)* Hi! How's it going?

ABBY. Look, it's just that —

MICHAEL. Donovan Cooper stayed in my room.

ABBY. Yes, he did.

MICHAEL. I read that. In the *binder.*

ABBY. It was years ago. Before he was famous. He wrote "The Cliffs of Eden" in that room. You've read that, I'm sure.

MICHAEL. Better yet, I saw the movie. In fact, I've seen all his books and never had to read a word he's written. I so admire those authors who lean right into the gaping maw of pop culture; those titans of literary commerce who do everything short of actually sucking you off and spitting your cum into a towel.

(She stares at him.)

MICHAEL. *(Cont'd.)* I have *issues.*

ABBY. I see that.

MICHAEL. I'm a snob. I'm proud of that. It means I have standards. It means I have not been aesthetically gentrified into making up-market pabulum for the typical beach-reading drone.

ABBY. *(Enjoying this.)* It means you don't sell any books.

MICHAEL. It means that, too.

ABBY. Donovan Cooper's novels have been translated into fifteen languages.

MICHAEL. That's great.

ABBY. Yes, it is.

MICHAEL. I hope they keep it up until they find a language he can *write in.*

ABBY. He's articulate, he's prolific, he's popular —

MICHAEL. He's on your Board of Directors —

ABBY. That has nothing to do with —

MICHAEL. *(Overlapping.)* And somewhere he's got a dozen grad students — locked in a basement — living on Gummy Bears and Diet Cokes — and twice a year, like clockwork, they crank out a book for him.

ABBY. Do you really think that someone who sells a book to the movies is suddenly a lesser writer?

MICHAEL. Abby, do you know why film is called a "medium"? Because it is neither *rare* nor *well-done.*

ABBY. I bet your books are as trite as you are.

MICHAEL. Oh, my books are worse.

ABBY. And *that* — that *faux humility* — that is really obnoxious. Just once I'd like to ask a writer who their favorite author is and have them say: "Me. I'm the writer I most like to read."

MICHAEL. Oh, you can find those writers. They're called "professors."

ABBY. What do you write about?

(He stares at her.)

ABBY. *(Cont'd.)* Hey. I'll bite. What is the crux of your important work that will never be made into a movie?

MICHAEL. Your friends are waiting.

ABBY. Yes, they are.

(Silence. She stares at him, waiting.)

MICHAEL. Like most men of my age and station, I wish only to write about two things: Injustice. And women. And while many of us

FICTION

claim to write about the former — we're all just writing about the latter. A war erupts, sure, that's terrible; poverty and famine scorch the earth, I know, I empathize; man blunders forth, lost and alone, a tiny stick figure in the cold eye of god, right, these are noble and burning questions... *but have you ever seen the way a woman pulls back her hair when she's about to get a drink of water from a fountain?* At that moment, you don't want to write a sentence that will change the world. Right then, you can have the Constitution, the Bill of Rights, and the fucking Magna Carta — just give me one glimpse of *that.*

(She stares at him.)

    ABBY. Tell me.
    MICHAEL. Hmm?
    ABBY. Tell me something you've written.

(He stares at her. Then ...)

    MICHAEL. "Whenever she appeared, I felt I had not an enemy in the world. I glowed with a flame of charity which moved me to forgive all who had ever injured me. And if at that moment someone had asked me a question, about anything, my only reply would have been: 'Love.'"

(He takes a long swig of his drink. Silence.)

    ABBY. Nice.
    MICHAEL. Thanks.
    ABBY. Dante.
    MICHAEL. You know it?
    ABBY. You prefer that I don't?
    MICHAEL. No, I just —
    ABBY. So you can pass it off as your own?
    MICHAEL. I wouldn't — I mean, I *couldn't* —

ABBY. Oh, right.

MICHAEL. It's too well known.

ABBY. I see.

MICHAEL. I mean, what do you take me for?

ABBY. But you have, right?

MICHAEL. Passed his words — the words of Dante! — off as my own?

ABBY. Mm hmm.

MICHAEL. Oh, sure. Dozens of times.

ABBY. I see.

MICHAEL. You seldom get called out on Dante. People will always nail you on Shakespeare or Yeats or even on some infantile nonsense by Rilke — but change a pronoun here and there and Dante's got a nice little *linquistic stealth* to him — you can just *ease him on in there* —

ABBY. Right.

MICHAEL. — and you're just WAITING for the chance to leave.

ABBY. Yes, I am.

MICHAEL. I have a request. Some things I need in my cottage.

ABBY. Just let the interns know — they'll take care of it.

MICHAEL. It's a bit unconventional — I'm not sure the interns can provide what I need.

ABBY. You'd be surprised. *(A loaded beat.)* They're *very eager*.

(He stares at her.)

ABBY. *(Cont'd.)* I liked the water fountain thing. That was nice.

MICHAEL. Thank you.

ABBY. Who wrote that?

MICHAEL. George Meyer.

ABBY. I'll check him out.

(And she is gone.)

FICTION

LINDA. And then, in the journal, he returns to Dante ...
MICHAEL. *(Looking off.)* "My strange illusion then I put aside ...
LINDA. ... Calling the name of her for whom I had sighed."

*(**Home**. She closes the journal. Then, she looks up at the audience.)*

LINDA. A secret, like a disease, is a very... human thing. It hides inside you. Discovers where you are most vulnerable. And then it hurts you. Only something with a heart could treat you like that.

*(She re-opens the journal. Turns a page. **The Cottage**. Day.)*

MICHAEL. Day Two. The Drake Colony. I have written exactly five words today. They are: *(Reads from his journal.)* "Day. Two. The. Drake. Colony." *(Sets journal down.)* I imagine the flurry of work in all the other cottages; all those productive little fuckers filling up pages with their deadening heart-felt drivel. Or worse, much worse: what if they are writing *well*? This hurts me where I live. As a writer, I am really only good at two things: *envy* and *criticism*. And the thought that someone — anyone — is actually writing something of value — something they will smugly lord over me as we make chit chat tonight, over dinner, at Poppy's House — that thought alone should be enough to hurl me back into work of my own. *(Beat.)* But it doesn't. Because I don't like to write. I like to *have written*.

(ABBY appears. She is carrying a box of painting supplies.)

ABBY. I think it's all here.
MICHAEL. The blue tape?
ABBY. Yes.
MICHAEL. Gotta have my blue tape. And my little foam brushes — love those. And the Beatles?

(She hands him a cassette tape.)

> ABBY. "Twist and Shout."
> MICHAEL. I'm a happy man.

(He is busy unpacking the box; perhaps throwing a drop cloth over the desk. He sees that she is not leaving.)

> MICHAEL. *(Cont'd.)* Thanks a lot.
> ABBY. Okay ...
> MICHAEL. See you later.

(She does not leave. He continues his preparations.)

> ABBY. I've got to ask.
> MICHAEL. "Whatever you need in your cottage. Whatever will allow you to do your work."
> ABBY. Yes, right —
> MICHAEL. It says that IN THE BINDER.
> ABBY. But *painting supplies?*
> MICHAEL. Donovan Cooper stayed in this room.
> ABBY. Yes —
> MICHAEL. No, listen, carefully: he *created* in here.
> ABBY. What does that —
> MICHAEL. Abby, this room needs to be *purged*. It requires a full *ritual cleansing* — top to bottom, scrubbed, sanded and painted. After that we'll burn a butt-load of sage and maybe get a shaman in here to give it the spiritual once-over.
> ABBY. You're serious.
> MICHAEL. I care about literature. It's the least I can do. *(Re: the can of paint.)* What color did you say we got?
> ABBY. "Pennywhistle."
> MICHAEL. Pennywhistle?! Wouldn't you love to be the Guy Who

FICTION

Names The Paint? Do you know what he's called? — of course, you don't because your head is not yet filled with needless conversational trivia — but, just FYI: he's called the *Swatch Bard.* I love that. And what, pray tell, must be the Swatch Bard's qualifications: experience with hallucinogenics and a thesaurus? "*Pennywhistle*" — I just love it.

ABBY. You're that stuck, huh?

(He stares at her, motionless. Then, he busies himself once again.)

ABBY. *(Cont'd.)* It happens. Writers come here and get stuck. The lack of distractions is often the greatest distraction of all.

MICHAEL. Not for me. My distraction is not nearly so vague.

(She stares at him. He looks up from his work.)

MICHAEL. *(Cont'd.)* May I tell you what it is?
ABBY. By all means.

(He is close to her. He seems about to tell her ... then, eyes still on her, he changes the subject.)

MICHAEL. Your last name is Drake. I just figured that out.
ABBY. You're a quick one.

MICHAEL. And "Poppy's House" — he was your grandfather — Henry Drake. You grew up here.

ABBY. Yes.

MICHAEL. So, why did you stay? When the foundation took it over — when it became a writer's retreat. It's not your home anymore — why stick around?

ABBY. That's really none of your —

MICHAEL. *(With an edge.)* I mean, why muck about with the likes of me? Why not ride your little trust fund away to the Hamptons or Vail or the Isle of Capri? I mean, clock's-a-tickin', baby — you're gettin' a little *ripe* to play the debutante, don't you think?

    ABBY. *(Ticked off.)* You are such a —

(Stops, thinks better of it.)

    MICHAEL. *(Challenging her.)* What?
    ABBY. Never mind.

(She starts to leave.)

    MICHAEL. Oooooooh, we made it to the edge there, didn't we?!

(This stops her.)

    MICHAEL. *(Cont'd.)* Good for us. Things don't get interesting until someone says "never mind." Then they're right on the precipice of saying what they really want to say. *(Insistent, a dare.)* C'mon, Abby. Take another step. You're almost there —
    ABBY. You'd like that, wouldn't you? —
    MICHAEL. You rich girls are the same way in bed —
    ABBY. *(And out it comes.) You smug little pathetic fraud.*

(This lands. MICHAEL smiles.)

    MICHAEL. Feel better now? You look better. Truth is the ultimate makeover.
    ABBY. Doesn't seem to help you.
    MICHAEL. Ouch.
    ABBY. Goodbye, Mr. Waterman.

(She goes.)

    MICHAEL. *(Sharp.)* Off to fawn over your other writers?

(She does not stop. And he does not stop talking.)

MICHAEL. *(Cont'd.)* I guess that's why you stick around. You're a — let's see, what's a nice word for it? — you're a bit of an *Art Tart.* A *Novelist-Chaser.* A sort of *Literary Leech*. Am I right?!

(Silence.)

MICHAEL. *(Cont'd.)* I know you're right outside the door. I know you want to have the last word. And hey, I'll let you. Come back in and — I promise — you can have the last word.

(She steps back into the room.)

ABBY. At least your wife knows how to write.

(She stares at him. Waits for him to say something. He looks at her. He "buttons" his lips with his fingers. She leaves. He turns to the audience.)

MICHAEL. "Achingly vibrant." *(Pause.)* You see, it turns out I had written those words after all. But not about my wife. *(Off, in the direction Abby left.)* About her.
LINDA. *(Knowingly, to audience.)* Okay: how long, do you think? How many pages before it happens?

(She pages through the journal.)

LINDA. *(Cont'd.)* Three?
MICHAEL. *(Journal entry.)* Finished sanding. First coat of primer on ...
LINDA. *(Turns more pages.)* Five?

FICTION

MICHAEL. *(As before.)* Okay — it might just be the fumes, but I'm beginning to really bond with this "Pennywhistle." Now, for the trim, I'm torn between "Serenity" and "Moonmist" —

LINDA. Ten?

MICHAEL. Almost no one can write about sex.

LINDA. Ah. Here we go ...

MICHAEL. Attraction, seduction, afterglow — sure, no problem — these are fiction's stock-in-trade. But when serious writers try to turn fleshy geometric repetition into words, it always comes out sounding like a bad nature show —

LINDA. *(Overlapping from "words".)* Alright, already. Get on with it, Michael —

MICHAEL. And so, dear reader, I cannot write about yesterday afternoon.

LINDA. Oh, the hell you can't —

MICHAEL. I can only say that we both had seen it coming for several days.

LINDA. *(Turning pages back.)* Going *back* a few days ...

MICHAEL. It was pouring rain. Her hair was wet. And we were talking about *apocope*. I told her that's how she got from Abigail to Abby. The dropping of the final sound from the end of a word: apocope.

*(**The Cottage.** Night. ABBY has entered. She holds a bottle of red wine and two juice glasses.)*

ABBY. It's a nickname. "Abby." It's just a —

MICHAEL. Yes, but there's a *word* for it. For the *act* of it. And that word is apocope.

(She stares at him. Pours some wine.)

MICHAEL. *(Cont'd. With a laugh.)* What?

ABBY. You have a knack for complication.

FICTION

MICHAEL. Do I?

ABBY. Tonight at dinner you talked about "the manner in which the apex of that structure was illuminated."

MICHAEL. Well, it was.

ABBY. *The top of the building was lit.*

MICHAEL. It deserved better.

ABBY. It was a gas station.

MICHAEL. Even so.

ABBY. I never heard a table of writers get so quiet.

MICHAEL. At least I didn't tell my joke.

(She stares at him. Waiting.)

MICHAEL. *(Cont'd.)* Is that a dare?

ABBY. Sure. Call it a dare.

MICHAEL. Husband and wife in bed. Late at night. Phone rings. Wife answers it. Pauses for a moment, listening. Then, a bit put-out, she says: "How should I know? That's a thousand miles from here." She hangs up. Man says: "Who was that?" "I don't know" says the wife, "some woman. She wanted to know if the coast was clear."

(MICHAEL stares at her. Waiting.)

ABBY. It's funny —

MICHAEL. Thank you.

ABBY — that you went with the "Moonmist." *(Beat.)* You were leaning toward "Serenity."

MICHAEL. I couldn't make my peace with it.

ABBY. I see.

MICHAEL. Odd for me.

ABBY. Really?

MICHAEL. I can usually make my peace with anything.

ABBY. That's a skill.

FICTION

MICHAEL. Yes, it is.

ABBY. Can you make your peace with *this?*

(Silence. She is staring at him.)

MICHAEL. What changed?

ABBY. Hmm?

MICHAEL. The last few days. What happened? I lost my ability to insult you —

ABBY. Oh, I doubt that.

MICHAEL. To piss you off until you storm away?

ABBY. Do people use you?

MICHAEL. What?

ABBY. To get to your wife?

MICHAEL. *(A bit thrown.)* Well, I don't —

ABBY. Her book is so remarkable — it grabbed me from Page One: *"His name was Simon. He was from Soweto. He invited me to a party."*

MICHAEL. She'd be honored that you're quoting her.

ABBY. And so lovely. So poised and articulate — her face plastered hither and yon.

MICHAEL. The "Flavor of the Month" she would say.

ABBY. No — she's the real deal. The moment I started "At the Cape" I could tell.

MICHAEL. She wrote that here, you know. *(His tone grows more intimate.)* She'd told *no one* that story. Not even me. Wrote it all in a mad rush. The night before she sent it to her publisher, she came to me, eyes red with tears. And she put a copy in my hands.

(She moves close to him.)

ABBY. So, do they? Use you to get close to her?

MICHAEL. Not that I know of.

ABBY. Oh, you'd know.

(She removes his wine glass from his hand. Sets it aside.)

MICHAEL. I guess you're the first.

(She touches his face with her fingers.)

MICHAEL. *(Cont'd.)* Would you like to meet her?
ABBY. *(Simply.)* I've met her.

(Puts her fingers on his lips.)

ABBY. *(Cont'd.)* She wouldn't remember me.
LINDA. *(Quietly.)* And here... I imagine they kiss.

(They do not kiss.)

MICHAEL. *(Quietly.)* I'll mention you've read her book.
ABBY. *(Quietly.)* One page.
MICHAEL. Hmm?
ABBY. That's all it took. Just *one page.*
LINDA. And here ... I imagine the rest.

*(**Home.** LINDA closes the journal.)*

LINDA. I sit in the darkened room. Then: a car in the drive. It shudders to a stop and is silent. Black shoes crunching gravel on the path. Keys out. One, two — click, turn, open — three, four — the hinge creaks as it closes — five, six — keys fall on the front table — coins from a pocket — seven, eight, nine steps into the room ...

(MICHAEL stands, looking at her. She meets his eye.)

MICHAEL. Sorry.

(She stares at him.)

MICHAEL. *(Cont'd.)* I stayed away as long as I could.

(Lights rush to black.)

End of Act One

ACT TWO

*(**Home.** Night. The image — MICHAEL and LINDA with coffee cups in front of them — is similar to the opening of the play. The tone, however, is not. There is an extremely long, silent moment in which they stir, sip, cradle, ignore their coffees. They do not look at one another. Nearby is the wooden box. The ground all around it is littered with dozens and dozens of MICHAEL's journals. Finally...)*

LINDA. Roger called.
MICHAEL. Hmm?
LINDA. Your agent. You have an agent named Roger.
MICHAEL. He called?
LINDA. Mm hmm.

(Silence.)

LINDA. *(Cont'd.)* Do you want to know why?
MICHAEL. Sure.
LINDA. I mean, if you don't —
MICHAEL. No, sure, that's fine —
LINDA. If you don't want to know, that's fine with me —
MICHAEL. If it's important, then, sure, I'd —
LINDA. Oh, it's important. Are you kidding?! I answered because I

thought it might be you — or my doctor — or one of my students. But, no — this was *Roger*. This was *important.*

MICHAEL. And?

LINDA. Bingo. Boffo. Big Bucks Blockbuster.

MICHAEL. What the —

LINDA. Your new book — the book you haven't even finished writing — it just went for the biggest advance Warner Brothers has ever paid. More than double your last book. And the best part — Roger was giddy about this — Variety is saying you have now "supplanted Donovan Cooper as the novelist Hollywood most desires." Isn't that great?!

MICHAEL. Linda —

LINDA. He went on and on — I jotted down some notes — they're on your desk —

MICHAEL. Enough, okay —

LINDA. Something about that actress who was in that HBO thing we taped but never watched — the one married to that guy in the band who played at that benefit we didn't go to — anyway, I don't remember her name, but she has real tits and legs for days and she's just *dying to be in your movie.*

MICHAEL. If you want to have it out, let's have it out —

LINDA. Okay.

MICHAEL. Let's do it and be done with it —

LINDA. Okay.

MICHAEL. And then maybe we can —

LINDA. Yes?

MICHAEL. *(Very agitated, very lost.)* Maybe if we — I don't know — maybe then, after that, we can...

(He stops. Spent. Nothing there. LINDA just stares at him. After a moment, she goes to the piles of journals and lifts a small stack of five or six of them. Brings these few journals to the table. Sets them on the table in front of MICHAEL.)

FICTION

LINDA. These few journals here... do you know what they have in common?

MICHAEL. *(The truth.)* No.

LINDA. These are the journals that *do not* mention Abby Drake. These few alone are free of her. The rest — *(Looking at all the other journals.)* — well... you know. *(The stack in front of her.) These* I really enjoyed. I'd get 'em to Roger. Might be a movie in there.

(Silence.)

LINDA. *(Cont'd.)* You have *nothing to say?*

(Silence.)

MICHAEL. It never happened.

LINDA. *(Hard.)* Oh, really?

MICHAEL. Any of it.

LINDA. *(Re: the journals.)* It's all *there,* Michael — it's all there in *black and white!*

MICHAEL. I made it up. It's all lies —

LINDA. Oh, *give me a little credit* — I know the truth when I read it.

MICHAEL. Linda —

LINDA. *I forgave you.* That's the worst part. I read about your month together at the Drake — how it pained you to say goodbye and come home to me. And I closed that book — and I clenched my teeth — and I cried my damn eyes out — and I *forgave you.* Do you see? I sat here and I knew — with certainty — that you are bigger than any mistakes you've made — any things you've kept from me — and I wasn't about to throw that all away on some stupid fling with a woman at a writer's colony. *(Pause.) Damn* that felt good. I couldn't WAIT for you to get home so I could tell you how goddamn EVOLVED I am. I will tell you, Michael Waterman, that when I closed that journal I loved you more than the day

I married you. *(Pause.)* And so I ran a bath. Put on music. Brought a few more journals in with me, to read in the tub. Just to be near you. *(Beat, the rage comes out.)* And there she was. A year later. Two years. Three. Five. You and I barely got a mention in those pages. But Abby Drake ... you tracked her like a prized animal. I got out of the tub — ran for more of the books — dripping water all over our floors — pushing through to the recent years ... LAST YEAR... *THIS* YEAR... and she was still *right there. (Beat.)* Correction: Here. She was still right *here.*

MICHAEL. Linda —
LINDA. *I had forgiven you.*

(Long silence.)

LINDA. *(Cont'd.)* Small blessings.

(He looks at her.)

LINDA. *(Cont'd.)* To learn this now. At the end. We won't have to accommodate it. Watch it hover in this house. Have it play out in the courtroom of our friends. Lucky, really. To die with this news... rather than having to live with it. *(Pause, quieter.)* I couldn't do it, Michael? Could you? *(Silence.)*

(She moves to the table. Sits across from him. They do not look at each other. Finally, they speak to the audience.)

MICHAEL. For the rest of that night —
LINDA. We moved through the house with a sort of ...
MICHAEL. ... Calm.
LINDA. I don't know why, really.
MICHAEL. The worst was out.
LINDA. What more could we do?
MICHAEL. Over the next few weeks, the pain and the hurt —

FICTION

LINDA. The land mines of the past —
MICHAEL. They did not vanish —
LINDA. But, instead —
MICHAEL. They grew quiet.
LINDA. They *stood away.*
MICHAEL. Until all that remained was her illness ...
LINDA. ... And the waiting.

(Silence.)

MICHAEL. *(Turning to her.)* I asked if there was somewhere I could take her; any final place she'd love to go.
LINDA. Nowhere.
MICHAEL. — She said.

(He looks at her. She gives him a kind smile.)

LINDA. Nowhere at all.

(LINDA goes. MICHAEL is alone.)

MICHAEL. I stared at my journals. Poured a drink. Lit a fire. Then, I sat down and read the worst of them — the very worst — the most arrogant and damning and demeaning of them — I sat and rubbed my face right in the muck of it. And then I watched them burn. The fire was glad to have them. The smoke raced up and out of our home... vanishing with abandon.

(LINDA appears behind him.)

LINDA. Don't forget the page you tore out. The one I couldn't see.
MICHAEL. Oh, right.

FICTION

(MICHAEL produces this page from his pocket.)

    LINDA. May I?

(He stares at her. He nods. Hands her the piece of paper. She unfolds it. Looks at it.)

    LINDA. *(Cont'd.)* It's empty.

(She looks up at him. He says nothing.)

    LINDA. *(Cont'd.)* Why?
    MICHAEL. *(Quietly.)* I wanted you to imagine the worst.
    LINDA. *(Also quietly.)* Which I did.

(Pause. A long look at him.)

    LINDA. *(Cont'd.)* And the worst did not happen.

*(**Morning.** ABBY appears. Sees MICHAEL and LINDA. Silence. Standoff. MICHAEL between the two women trying to find the words to say. Finally —)*

    MICHAEL. I... uh... think you've met. Some years ago.
    LINDA. Yes.

(Silence.)

    ABBY. If this... I hope you'll tell me if this is...
    LINDA. A *bad time?*
    MICHAEL. Maybe we should —
    LINDA. Michael?
    MICHAEL. Hmm?

LINDA. Make us some tea.

(MICHAEL looks at her, then goes. The women are alone.)

ABBY. I just recently heard the news... about your illness.

LINDA. Did you?

ABBY. I forget where. I got an e-mail — or there was something in the paper —

LINDA. Right, whatever.

ABBY. And I didn't hear all the details, but I thought to myself...

(Stops.)

LINDA. *Good riddance?* Something like that?

ABBY. No.

(Silence.)

LINDA. He didn't know you were coming?

ABBY. No.

(Silence.)

LINDA. I've been reading about you. Seems you had a lovely trip to Paris. Here I was so worried that Michael would be stuck in days of meetings with those French film people — but apparently he was able to squeeze in a little pleasure on the side.

ABBY. Linda —

LINDA. He took you to the cafe where he and I met.

ABBY. Yes.

LINDA. How nice.

ABBY. It was something he wanted to do.

LINDA. What did you order? *(Before ABBY can respond.)* He didn't write that down. Not that he would. Michael's not big on food. Me — I love to eat. Him — he loves to *have eaten.*

(Silence. They are now seated at the table.)

    LINDA. *(Cont'd.)* So... you never read my book?
    ABBY. Does that surprise you?

(Silence.)

    LINDA. You know, when "At the Cape" was first published —
    ABBY. I didn't come here to listen to your stories.
    LINDA. *(Sharp.)* Well, you know, baby, that's the *price of admission.* You want to come visit my husband in the house he shares with me — well, hey, that's gonna cost you.
    ABBY. I came to *see you. (Pause, simply.)* To say goodbye.
    LINDA. *(Pause.)* Well, your timing stinks. Turns out I'm not going anywhere.

(MICHAEL reappears, with tea. Sets it between them.)

    MICHAEL. *(Brightly.)* They're calling it an "oncological misapprehension."
    LINDA. A screw up.
    MICHAEL. *(The good news gushes out.)* The doctors are citing "a confluence of mitigating factors" which repeatedly produced a "false positive" — a sort of "shadow malignancy" — when, in fact, the last MRI showed a diminishment — *a profound diminishment* of —
    LINDA. My little storm troopers are diving in and kicking some ass.
    MICHAEL. She'll start a new round of chemotherapy next week — which has its own risks, of course, but nothing like what we've been up against to this point. After that, we hope — we assume — she'll be back

teaching. And, of course, writing. *(To LINDA.)* Don't we?

(LINDA gives him no response. He turns to ABBY.)

    MICHAEL. *(Cont'd.)* Isn't that something?
    ABBY. It's great.
    LINDA. Oh, it's *so great.* Now I get to *live with this.*

(MICHAEL stares at the two women, then turns and speaks to the audience.)

    MICHAEL. As I looked around the room: *the color of the walls had changed.* The floors were foreign to me; the furniture transformed. Out the window, a landscape bleak as the moon. And there, sitting in two chairs, facing one another... there were the architects of this strange new place. I set the tea between them. Poured them each a cup. The clatter of tiny spoons; the swirling, scented steam. And, finally, Linda's voice ...
    LINDA. Michael.
    MICHAEL. Hmm?
    LINDA. Make up the guest room. Abby is going to spend the night.

(ABBY looks at LINDA. MICHAEL turns to the audience.)

    MICHAEL. We found ourselves at a restaurant. Garish smiles from the wait staff. The food perfect on the plate; tasteless on the tongue. Next: a book store. Linda's idea. She lead Abby to the section filled with my novels. Abby inquired about "At the Cape." I prayed the night would end. Abby suggested a jazz club she'd read about. Linda was all for it. I dropped them off and parked the car. When I stepped inside, they were sitting in a back booth. Each staring at the stage. Not saying a word. The band was between sets. The only person onstage was the drummer — he was adjusting the pedal of his high-hat; tightening the heads on a set of toms. Linda and Abby *watched his every move* — transfixed. And from where I stood I could read Linda's lips. She said ...

LINDA. *(To ABBY.)* I'm sorry.

(ABBY turns to LINDA.)

MICHAEL. When I reached the table, the music began — and they said they were ready to go. We made it home. Said our "good nights" like it was the most normal thing in the world. Linda took her pills, washed her face, climbed into bed with a book — every ritual intact. I sat in bed next to her — *my thoughts so loud I was certain she could hear them.* Soon she closed her book and kissed my cheek. Her light went off... And I thought of Abby. In our guest room, downstairs. *Why on earth had she come?* It wasn't to see me — it couldn't have been — she'd barely spoken to me... And now I am stepping out of my bed. I am walking slowly down the stairs — skipping over the fourth one, the noisy one — what the emperors would have called the "nightingale." Abby's room is dark; the door slightly ajar. Ten steps down the hall and I am there, standing at the threshold. Pushing open the door — a ghost in my own home —

LINDA. She's gone.

(LINDA is behind him.)

LINDA. *(Cont'd.)* Said to tell you goodbye. You'd already gone upstairs — we didn't want to disturb you.

MICHAEL. What was this? This *thing we did tonight?!*

LINDA. She's nice, don't you think?

MICHAEL. *Jesus,* Linda —

LINDA. I mean, sure, there's this little matter of *serial deception* — we'll have to work through that — but, hey —

MICHAEL. *(Strong.)* It's over.

LINDA. Uh-huh.

MICHAEL. It's *long over.*

FICTION

LINDA. Enough —

MICHAEL. It's been over for *years* —

LINDA. — *I don't want to hear it.*

MICHAEL. *(Overlapping.)* Listen to me! We did meet in Paris.

LINDA. Yes, I read that, Michael. Sorry about all the *rain.*

MICHAEL. I was there on business —

LINDA. Quote, unquote.

MICHAEL. And she was returning by train from Avignon —

LINDA. How convenient.

MICHAEL. And we arranged to meet.

LINDA. *(Sharp.)* And let me guess *where*:

*(A **Cafe Table**. ABBY ENTERS.)*

ABBY. *(With a definite edge.)* The *Cafe Rue Cler*?

MICHAEL. You found it.

ABBY. Why would you bring me here?!

MICHAEL. Listen —

ABBY. Do you know how hard it is to do something UNROMAN-TIC in Paris? This city is one big satin sheet. But, you, Michael, have risen to the occasion.

MICHAEL. Will you please let me —

ABBY. *Bringing me to the cafe where you met your wife?!* You should be — I don't know — written up or something. It's really unbelievable.

MICHAEL. Coffee?

ABBY. *Wine.*

MICHAEL. *(Edgy.)* Wine it is. Coming right up.

(He joins her at the table. Looks around for a waiter. Snaps fingers. Anxious. She just stares at him. Finally, he meets her gaze.)

MICHAEL. *(Cont'd.)* You're soaking wet.

ABBY. *(Direct.)* Once you liked me that way.

(Silence.)

    MICHAEL. *(Looks at her, shakes his head.)* God ... these meetings ...

    ABBY. Yes ...?

    MICHAEL. Pointless. Every one of them.

    ABBY. Michael —

    MICHAEL. All these producers want to have long talks about "art" and "cinema" and the "cultural moment" — they want to do ANYTHING but actually recognize that we are talking about A MOVIE — a movie we ALL know how to make — a movie we ALL have made before — a movie in which the pretty girl is in love and then in danger and then in her underwear.

    ABBY. Which book is this? I lose track.

    MICHAEL. Does it matter?

    ABBY. So bitter.

    MICHAEL. I'm a hack.

    ABBY. A *popular* hack.

    MICHAEL. Okay, that hurts. *(Beat.)* I'm sorry about this place. I just needed something familiar.

(She looks away. Silence.)

    MICHAEL. *(Cont'd.)* You look great.

    ABBY. *(Immediate, direct.)* Why now? *(Pause.) Nothing.* For *years.* And then: this. *(Pause.)* She found out. You finally told her?

    MICHAEL. No. I thought about telling her, years ago —

    ABBY. When there was something to tell?

    MICHAEL. Yeah — I suppose — but, now, what would I say?

    ABBY. Tell her the *truth*. You had a fling at a writer's retreat. You spent a *month* with another woman and then *you never saw her again.* Hey, that's what those places are for. Everybody knows that. At the beginning of all these books, when the writer says: "I'd like to thank the Whatever Colony for their support" — what do you think they're saying "thank you" FOR? The desk? The food? The fresh air? *Please*.

MICHAEL. Abby —

ABBY. I never even *heard,* Michael. Two letters, a phone call. In what? — *a dozen years?*

MICHAEL. We've been busy.

ABBY. I see.

MICHAEL. You and I.

(Pause. She looks at him, confused.)

ABBY. What are you talking about?

MICHAEL. *(Pause, with passion.)* We've spent long weekends together. Trips to Venice, Prague, the Isle of Skye. That dumb little junket to Atlantic City. And best of all, our road trip down the Oregon coast. My favorite of them all. That tiny cabin perched over the water. Sleeping on the deck. Sharing our lunch with the gulls.

(She stares at him. He comes clean.)

MICHAEL. *(Cont'd.)* I've been inventing you since the day we met. Between the pages of my journals, I am Dante and you are my Beatrice. *La Vita Nuova.*

(Silence.)

ABBY. I need that wine now.

MICHAEL. Abby, listen —

ABBY. *(Sharp.)* You don't know me. You don't know a *thing* about me.

MICHAEL. No, I don't. It's just —

ABBY. *What?*

MICHAEL. — "the innocent ecstasy of the unattainable."

ABBY. More Dante?

MICHAEL. No — I'm afraid that's me.

ABBY. Well, what do you know? *An original thought.* Not your strong suit, is it?

MICHAEL. I think I've admitted as much.

ABBY. Same with your wife. Did you ever think — the two of you — did you ever consider that maybe you should have made *children,* instead of books? Something genuine and tangible that might look you in the eye and call your bluff. But oh, no — not the two of you. *You thrive on your fictions.*

MICHAEL. Abby —

ABBY. No. You want to talk to me?: go home and *make up what I said.* You're good at that. *(ABBY leaves.)*

*(**Home.** Night. LINDA approaches ABBY, holding a few folded towels.)*

LINDA. Here are towels for you. There's a spare robe on the back of the door, if you need it. I have treatment in the morning, so we'll be up early. Sorry if we wake you. These old houses — you hear everything.

ABBY. I'm not staying. You know that. *(LINDA stares at her.)*

ABBY. *(Cont'd.)* I liked that club. Watching that drummer.

LINDA. Yes.

ABBY. I knew exactly what you were thinking.

(Silence.)

ABBY. *(Cont'd.) I forgive you, Linda.*

LINDA. *(Pause.)* That's what you came to say? *(ABBY nods.)*

LINDA. *(Cont'd.)* I made it easy for you, didn't I? — to sleep with my husband? Gave you a nice clean chance to get back at me.

ABBY. Linda —

LINDA. Or are you gonna be like Michael and tell me none of it

ever happened?!
    ABBY. *(Pause.)* No.
    LINDA. Thank you.

(LINDA stares at her. Then, she hands ABBY something which has been hidden amid the towels. It is a diary.)

    LINDA. *(Cont'd.)* This is for you. I should have done this years ago.

(ABBY looks at the diary — not opening it. Then, she looks back up at LINDA.)

    LINDA. *(Cont'd.)* It's all in there. Do what you want with it.

(ABBY stares at LINDA, then nods.)

    ABBY. Okay.

(ABBY starts to go —)

    LINDA. What should I tell Michael?
    ABBY. Whatever you'd like. *(ABBY is gone, taking the diary with her.)*

*(A **Classroom**. LINDA addressing her students.)*

    LINDA. And so, dear tortured young writers, it is there, in the final chapter of "At the Cape," that our young woman must come to grips with her life. And to do that, she must go see the *line.* That line of white water, trailing into the distance. The place where two worlds collide. *(A question is asked.)* "But, is the story really true?" asks — I always forget your name — *Suzanne.* "Like the Leonard Cohen song." Oh, thank you. That's so helpful. And Leonard Cohen — what an inspiration; a stirring reminder of how little it takes to be called a poet in America. *(With passion.)* The thing is, Suzanne: *Go there.* To the tip of Africa. The Cape of Good Hope — the place where Vasco da Gama planted his flag. And there you will see that line of water. Something like that cannot be invented. It simply *is. (Another question.)* Yes, my young friend of indeterminate gender: My *husband's* books — are they "true," as well? *(Smiles.)* That's a tough one. Michael's theory is "Why put yourself in your book?! People will *find you in your book* whether you're in there or not." *(Pause.)* Just for the record: my husband was not always a "hack." That is his word, mind you, not mine. Each day he rises early, goes into his office and closes the door "til it latches" — that is very important — he hates a door that is slightly ajar. He puts on what he calls "important music" — Elgar, Bartok, Schumann — to whose accompaniment he writes what he calls "the pre-emptive novelizations of my soon-to-be-forgettable movies." *(MICHAEL appears. He is holding an old, weathered apple box. It is filled to the brim with diaries of various sizes and colors.)* His first novel, though, has never gained wide acclaim. It will certainly never be filmed. And therefore, it remains my favorite. It is called "The Asterisk." A short novel about a man dealing with the loss of a friend. The plot is admittedly unremarkable. The language, however, is filled with music. And the conceit of the book — that which gives it it's name — I believe it is inspired. *(During the following, MICHAEL sets the apple box down in the room. Kneels. Stares down into it.)* In Michael's book, whenever the main character and his friend do something together, unknowingly, for the last time ... an *asterisk* appears in the margin. "They climbed in his car and made the drive into town." *Asterisk.* "And no sooner had he turned, but he saw the smile on his friend's face." *Asterisk.*

*(LINDA is gone. **Home.** MICHAEL looks up at the audience.)*

MICHAEL. It was Monday. A few weeks later. I was in my car. Driving to the store. In the movies, people's loved ones are always at the hospital; at their side till the very end. And everything — even the movie itself — seems to stop for a moment. For a reckoning. *(Pause.)* My cell phone rang. I listened and I wept and I drove. The lights changed. Cars moved through traffic. The world *did not stop*. We'd been warned that the chemo would weaken her — make her susceptible to pneumonia. The doctor reminded me of this. And then, by way of comforting me I guess, he told me Linda's death was, quote, *not remarkable at all. (Pause.)* At her memorial, I stood before friends and family. I stood, looking inside myself for the words. And, failing to find them, I lifted a line from Dante: *"Until this moment, heaven had but one imperfection ... the lack of her."*

(Silence. Then... MICHAEL lifts one of the diaries out of the box, as — LINDA appears. She is carrying a pen, and a diary which is identical to that which MICHAEL is reading from.)

LINDA. *(Joyous, a diary entry.)* Paris, like any first love, is both definitive and elusive. Its effect remembered, but never replicated.

MICHAEL. *(To the audience.)* A week later the phone rang. It was the University. Had I decided on a repository for Linda's papers?

LINDA. At the Tuilleries, an old woman feeding a sparrow in her hands.

MICHAEL. The University would be very interested in securing and cataloging her complete work —

LINDA. "It's a good path," she says.

MICHAEL. Her fiction —

LINDA. I nod.

MICHAEL. Her letters —

LINDA. "See how *slowly* everyone walks — that is the mark of a successful path."

MICHAEL. And most importantly: any *personal writings*, any *diaries* she may have left behind.

FICTION

(MICHAEL opens the diary.)

LINDA. *(Another entry, buoyant.)* I met him today. His name is Michael. And, shockingly, he is EVEN A GREATER SNOB THAN I —

MICHAEL. *(Overlapping.)* "Even a greater snob than I. We have very different tastes in art and music, literature and movies — but, thankfully, we HATE all the same things."

(MICHAEL smiles.)

LINDA. Pollock —
MICHAEL. "Hemingway" —
LINDA. Bergman —
MICHAEL. "The Beach Boys" —
LINDA. No bond is stronger than that of *ecstatically shared hatreds.* We also both hate "swing music." The music — as Michael says —

MICHAEL. *(To audience.)* — That everyone *dances to* because they can't bear to *listen to it.*

LINDA. He also believes it is a tragedy to put beer in a green bottle; and that a closed door must always be pulled until it latches.

*(MICHAEL smiles. He pulls another diary from the box, opens it and reads. **A Cottage.**)*

MICHAEL. *(Reading.)* "Day Five. The Drake Colony."

LINDA. *(Standing behind her desk, fierce and joyous.)* Huge progress. *Heaps* of work. Wilde said the first line of a poem falls from the ceiling. In my case, it is *raining* words; entire paragraphs and chapters. My working title is "At the Cape" and my hope is to —

(ABBY appears. Holding a manuscript.)

FICTION

ABBY. Hi.

LINDA. Oh, great. You got a chance to read it.

ABBY. Yes.

LINDA. The other writers are all swamped with their own work, I know — so that's why, when I told you I was working on a piece about South Africa, well, you seemed so *interested* — or maybe you were just being *polite* — oh, god, maybe *that was it — sorry — anyway*, you read it and I'm *thrilled* and — *hi* — it's Abby, right?

ABBY. Right.

LINDA. Hi. *(Beat.)* God. I'm sorry. I've been, just, you know, *cooped up in here* — this desk, these glaring white walls, the happy little binder — I don't know, Abby, I've just been *so hungry for* — *(She stops. Silence.)*

ABBY. *(Simply.)* Thanks for letting me read it.

(LINDA nods, avidly. ABBY sets the manuscript down in the room. Speaks, pleasantly.)

ABBY. *(Cont'd.)* If there's anything else you need, just let one of the interns know.

(She turns and starts off.)

LINDA. Whoa whoa whoa!

(ABBY stops.)

LINDA. *(Cont'd.)* That's it?

ABBY. Was there something else?

LINDA. Well — yes — I think so — I mean, just out of courtesy — I thought you could at least —

ABBY. What?

LINDA. I don't know.

ABBY. Praise you?

LINDA. That would do.

ABBY. Well, let's see, what will they call it? — a "coming of age" story. Set against "the dangerous and alluring backdrop of a foreign land."

LINDA. Thanks for turning my life into a blurb.

ABBY. It's good. It is.

LINDA. But?

ABBY. Please.

LINDA. BUT?

ABBY. Let's not do this.

LINDA. It's very good, BUT?

ABBY. *(Direct.)* It's not true. Not really. I mean — *is it? (Before LINDA can say more.)* Anyway: I don't believe it. Sorry. Other people, maybe most people will. You should ask them.

LINDA. Have you BEEN there?

ABBY. To South Africa?

LINDA. *To the Cape?*

ABBY. No.

LINDA. Then how dare you —

ABBY. Can we please not —

LINDA. *(Overlapping.)* I mean, if you've never BEEN THERE, really, how DARE YOU say something as —

ABBY. Meet me tonight.

LINDA. What?

ABBY. After dinner.

LINDA. Why the hell would I —

ABBY. Come out with us.

LINDA. No.

ABBY. Have a drink.

LINDA. No way in hell.

ABBY. Suit yourself.

LINDA. What time?

ABBY. Eight.

FICTION

LINDA. Don't count on it.
ABBY. See you then.
LINDA. Where?
ABBY. Ask around.

(And ABBY is gone.)

LINDA. *(An entry, edgy.)* And she was gone. And I couldn't wait to see her again. To *throttle* her. To break and convince her.

(MICHAEL looks up from the diary; speaks to the audience.)

MICHAEL. And after those words —
LINDA. To *win her over.*
MICHAEL. — The diary *ends.* I rummaged through the box. I read everything — all the diaries in a single night — I raced through them — looking for what happened next: her time at the Drake, with Abby, the days of finishing her book. But, *none of it was there.*

*(A **Bar.** ABBY approaches, carrying two beers.)*

ABBY. Brown bottles.
MICHAEL. You remembered.

(MICHAEL, his mood dark, just stares at her — not taking the beer.)

MICHAEL. *(Cont'd.)* So... to what do I owe?
ABBY. I wanted to see you. *(Pause.)* To tell you how sorry I am.

(MICHAEL says nothing.)

ABBY. *(Cont'd.)* I know how much you —
MICHAEL. You know: I guess I thought you'd be at Linda's memo-

rial.

ABBY. I heard it was lovely.

MICHAEL. I mean, it seems like you show up everywhere else —
at our *house,* in *her diaries* —

ABBY. Michael —

MICHAEL. *(Confused, angry.)* No — just let me say this while it's
still ME talking because soon enough it will be the BEER talking and,
hey, you'll like talking to the beer A LOT MORE than talking to ME —

ABBY. Would you please —

MICHAEL. *(Overlapping.)* — but, meanwhile, any-hoo, back at
Moot Point: you're SORRY? Well, okay, you know, far be it from me to
turn down anyone's *pity* — but that just won't *do,* Abby — that's not
good enough. Whatever happened, whatever went on between you and
my wife — *you did not know her.* Okay?! *You did not know her at all.*

(She stares at him for a moment.)

ABBY. I brought you something.

*(From her bag, ABBY produces the diary which LINDA gave to her. She
hands it to MICHAEL. He looks at it.)*

MICHAEL. This is Linda's.

*(MICHAEL opens the diary. LINDA ENTERS, purposefully. MICHAEL
does not see her. We are now in both bars — the past and the present
— simultaneously.)*

LINDA. "Ask around" — that's a great way to give directions.

ABBY. There are only two bars.

LINDA. I found the other one.

(LINDA takes the second beer bottle from ABBY.)

MICHAEL. *(To ABBY.)* How did you get this?

LINDA. *(Looking around, a dig.)* I see you have a lot of friends.

ABBY. *(Also a dig.)* How's the writing?

(MICHAEL steps away, reading from the diary, as — The women sit, drink their beers.)

LINDA. Terrific, thank you. I'm nearly done with my big ol' false Abby-Drake-doesn't-believe-a-word-of-it book. You're an inspiration, you really are.

ABBY. Thank you.

LINDA. I'm gonna finish it just to *piss you off.*

MICHAEL. Abby?

LINDA. And what's more: I resent how you blurbed me. A "coming of age" story — like it's "Little Women" goes to Africa.

ABBY. Well, isn't it? *(Before LINDA can respond.)* You want it re-blurbed? How's this?: "Girl goes to study abroad. Meets a man in Johannesburg. She trusts him. He rapes her. Buys her silence. Breaks her heart. She goes to the Cape. Looks at the water. Gets really sad and speaks in metaphors."

MICHAEL. *Abby —*

ABBY. Even if it happened, Linda, I just don't believe it *matters*.

LINDA. Hey — my life doesn't matter to you — fine. Yours doesn't matter a hell of a lot to me.

ABBY. *(Sharp.)* It would.

LINDA. What?!

ABBY. It would if you knew it.

MICHAEL. *Did she give this to you?!*

ABBY. You've been to the Cape — that much I believe.

LINDA. Thanks so much.

ABBY. But did he really try to BUY your silence? And was he really a "government official"? Oh, and better yet — given the regime he worked for — a GOOD government official? A NICE apartheid guy?!

LINDA. *(Sharp.)* Who just happened to *rape me*.

ABBY. Did he?!

LINDA. Yes.

ABBY. Linda —

LINDA. *Yes.*

(ABBY is eye to eye with LINDA. Her stare is strong, unforgiving.)

LINDA. *(Cont'd.)* Yes, he did.

(Pause.)

LINDA. *(Cont'd.)* His wife was away. He locked the door. And I was...

ABBY. Yes?

LINDA. ... *Coerced. (Pause.)* He ... took me ... and he ... *insisted.*

ABBY. And you fought him — gouged his back — kicked and screamed —

LINDA. *Yes.*

(ABBY continues to stare at her, hard.)

LINDA. *(Cont'd.)* Yes — I *wanted* to. I didn't want to be there. His wife... she'd been so... kind to me. But, I'd driven there that day — waited till she was gone — he invited me in. I was... *ashamed.*

ABBY. *(Quiet, firm.)* You wrote "raped."

LINDA. That's what it felt like.

ABBY. *There's a difference.*

LINDA. I don't have to do this, Abby —

ABBY. Just say it's not true!

LINDA. It's *TRUE ENOUGH.*

ABBY. *THANK YOU.*

LINDA. A true story does not make a book. A writer makes a book.

ABBY. Yeah — I've heard it all before —

LINDA. WHY DO YOU CARE, ANYWAY?

ABBY. *I was there a year ago.* In the townships. I never went to the Cape, though — you're right about that. I never got the chance.

LINDA. What are you talking about?!

ABBY. *Your story is not true.*

LINDA. And *YOURS IS?*

(ABBY says nothing, looks away.)

LINDA. *(Cont'd.)* C'mon, I gave you my story — you owe me a crack at yours.

(ABBY turns to LINDA. Leans in. Exacting a promise.)

ABBY. *No one.* Not my family. My friends. *No one knows this.* Do you understand?

(LINDA nods. A moment, then ... MICHAEL reads from the diary.)

MICHAEL. "Day Six. The Drake Colony. I have a *new story* for my book ..."

(A deep breath. And, slowly, she begins...)

ABBY. His name was Simon. He lived in Soweto. He invited me to a party. *(Pause.)* It was Sunday. I drove there alone — it was daylight, no worries— I went there to hear his band play.

MICHAEL. *(Reading.)* "A *shabeen,* they called it."

ABBY. A neighborhood party at a tiny cinder block house. Salty beer in old glass jars.

MICHAEL. "And Simon's band playing."

(ABBY's focus now turns to MICHAEL, as she says —)

ABBY. *(Nods.)* And Simon's band playing.

(Their eyes meet.)

MICHAEL. *(Making the connection.)* "He was a drummer ..."

(And now ABBY gives one final look to LINDA, saying —)

ABBY. *(Quietly.)* Yes.

(Silence, as —MICHAEL slowly closes the diary, and — ABBY watches LINDA stand... and leave.)

MICHAEL .Why bring me this now? If it's plagiarism — file a suit. I can't believe you didn't do that years ago.

ABBY. That's what my lawyer said. "Don't get on that plane. Don't go see him. And do not take that diary with you." I had to lie to him. Which is really kind of fun, actually — lying to your lawyer. It makes you feel *honest,* somehow.

MICHAEL. Abby —

ABBY. I *chose her*, Michael. Chose to tell her my story. *(Simply.)* And she told the *truth*.

(She walks up close to him.)

ABBY. *(Cont'd.)* What would Dante have to say about that?

(She walks past him and is gone. After a moment, MICHAEL turns to the audience.)

FICTION

MICHAEL. Linda's papers are now archived at the University. Her diaries are there, as well. *(Lifts the diary which ABBY gave to him.)* All but one. *(LINDA appears, opposite. Alone.)* Her final entries were written in the hospital:

LINDA. *(A diary entry.)* This place makes you do the damnedest things. Today, for some reason, I watched *horse racing.* Yes, *me.* I watched tiny men perched on saddles the size of coasters. I watched *horses* — creatures of such *bearing,* such *magnificence* they belong not on TV, but in stanzas by Dylan Thomas. And here's what happened: *I saw a horse jump over a shadow.* He's coming down the stretch — neck and neck with his rival — and the shadow of a flagpole or tower or something has fallen across the track. And this horse *jumps over it* — ruining his stride, allowing the rival horse to beat him by a nose. No one told him you don't jump a shadow. You just run through it. *(She moves and sits at the table.)* Michael here all day, god love him. And he brought music. Janis Joplin, cranked up loud — just to bug the nurses. And, I told him that — just for the record — he was STILL WRONG. We sat together, listening to that woman sing that song. *(beat, quietly) Asterisk. (Pause.)* Later, I started to drift off — thinking of Paris. I felt him cover me with the blanket. Heard his footsteps leave the room. Heard the door close. And latch.

*(A **Cafe Table.** MICHAEL approaches. LINDA is reading a newspaper.)*

MICHAEL. *(In badly mangled French.)* Pardon — Mademoiselle — Qu'est-ce que c'est? — Pouvez-vous me dire? — la table? — non, non — la chaise? — *occ-u-pied?*

(LINDA stares at him. Then —)

LINDA. Man, I thought *my* French was bad.
MICHAEL. You're American.
LINDA. *Oui.*

FICTION

(She returns to her paper. He stands there.)

    MICHAEL. This place is packed.
    LINDA. It's noon. People eat.
    MICHAEL. Nowhere to sit.

(She looks up at him.)

    LINDA. Nowhere at all.

(Again, she returns to her paper.)

    MICHAEL. What if ...?

(She looks up.)

    LINDA. Yes?
    MICHAEL. What if you said: "Join me?" Then, I'd say: "I don't want to trouble you." And you'd say: "No trouble at all." And I'd say: "Are you sure?" And you'd nod. And I'd sit and buy you a coffee. *(Beat.)* Or something.

(A moment. Just the two of them. Looking at one another.)

End of Play

FICTION

Author's note on Set Design for *Fiction*

It is necessary that this play is done, scenically, with great simplicity. The quick jumps in time and place which the text demands are possible only if this level of minimal scenery is employed and, in fact, exploited.

A central table can be used for the Café, the Drake Colony, the Bar, etc. A few chairs can be moved around the stage by the actors, as needed. Some productions have had a simple desk (or writing table) onstage, as well, to use for the scenes at the Drake Colony. This desk, however, was also incorporated into the blocking for the scenes at home, etc. — adding to the sense that the design of the play is based on "making a performing space" rather than "depicting a variety of locales."

There need be no "transitions" – rather, the story is driven by the actor and can change instantly upon the turn of a phrase; whatever else is required (a change in lighting, a simple prop) can follow from that.

There need be no set "dressing" – rather, any props that are called for can be carried both on and off by an actor in the scene.

FICTION

Costumes

<u>Linda</u>

Act One: Long skirt. Blouse. Comfortable shoes.
Add: Shawl or sweater (during "home" scene following medical diagnosis).

Act Two: Same.
Add: Colorful scarf (her dairy entries from Paris).
Add: Denim or leather jacket (going to bar to meet Abby).

<u>Michael</u>

Act One: Dark trousers. Sweater over casual shirt.
Add: Suede jacket ("going out" scene / Drake colony).

Act Two: Same.

<u>Abby</u>

Act One: Jeans. Light shirt. Sandals.
Add: Denim jacket ("bar" scene with Michael).
Add: Nicer blouse/shirt. Shoes. ("wine" scene with Michael).

Act Two: Skirt. Blouse/sweater. Dress boots. Nice jacket. Purse.
Restore: some part of Act One look (jeans, etc.) for scene with Linda at Drake Colony.
Restore: some part of early Act Two look (nice jacket, purse, etc.) for "double bar scene" with Michael/Linda.

FICTION

Props

Preset

2 coffee cups, saucers
French newspaper

Act One

Wooden ships' box (Michael)
Journals — Michael's, identical, enough to fill box
Shoulder bag — filled with pens, notebooks, etc. (Michael)
Clipboard and pencil (Abby)
Three-ring Binder (Abby)
Brown beer bottle (Michael)
Green beer bottle (Abby)
Box of painting supplies — brushes, blue tape, tarp (Abby)
Large can of paint — "pennywhistle" (Abby)
Smaller can of paint — in box with supplies (Abby)
Wine bottle (Abby)
2 glasses (Abby)

Act Two

Several dozen journals — Michael's (Preset)
2 coffee mugs (Preset)
2 tea cups and spoons (Michael)
Towels (Linda)
Diary — hidden in towels, distinctive look/color (Linda)
Apple box (Michael)
Diaries — Linda's, all shapes and colors and sizes, enough to fill apple box (Michael)
Diary — while in Paris (Linda)

FICTION

Diary — identical, being read by Michael
Manuscript — Linda's writing at Drake (Abby)
Pens, pencils, paper, etc. — on Linda's desk at Drake
2 beer bottles — brown (Abby)

Flight
ARTHUR GIRON

"A witty, touching flashback…There is poignancy
between the laughs." —*The New York Times*

The author doesn't claim it happened exactly this way. He has taken
real-life characters and biographical information and supposed what
it was like for Orville and Wilbur growing up in the dysfunctional
Wright family. They are portrayed as boys whose mischief is just a
sign of frustrated brilliance. Not a documentary, the play explores
the dynamics of the Wright family in theatrical terms. 4 m., 1 f.
(#8179)

Pride's Crossing
TINA HOWE

Best American Play of 1998
New York Drama Critics Circle
"A play you will remember and forever cherish.…It is rich in both
texture and imagination."— *New York Post*
"A lovely achievement…Mabel becomes a woman who … both
typified her time and her class and transcended it."—*Variety*

At ninety, Mabel Tidings Bigelow insists on celebrating her daugh-
ter and granddaughter's annual visit with a croquet party. As the
party unfolds, she relives vignettes from the past that reveal the
precise moment of opportunity lost and love rejected that define her
life. The vibrant portrait of Mabel that takes shape culminates in her
one shining achievement when she became the first woman to swim
the English Channel. 4 m., 3 f. (#18230)

**Send for your copy of the Samuel French
BASIC CATALOGUE OF PLAYS AND MUSICALS**